A TIME
FOR FIRES

Also by Vernon Scannell

A Mortal Pitch (1957)

Masks of Love (1960)
(*Heinemann Award for Literature, 1960*)

A Sense of Danger (1962)
(*Recommended by the Poetry Book Society*)

Walking Wounded (1965)

Epithets of War (1969)

Selected Poems (1971)

The Winter Man (1973)

The Loving Game (1975)
(*Poetry Book Society Choice*)

New & Collected Poems 1950-1980 (1980)

Winterlude (1982)

Funeral Games (1987)

Soldiering On (1989)

A TIME
FOR FIRES

poems by

VERNON
SCANNELL

Robson Books

First published in Great Britain in 1991 by

Robson Books Ltd,

Bolsover House,

5-6 Clipstone Street,

London W1P 7EB

British Library Cataloguing in Publication Data

Scannell, Vernon, 1922-
A time for fires.
I. Title
821.914
ISBN 0 86051 757 8

Designed by John Costelloe

Printed in Great Britain
by Billing & Sons ltd.,Worcester

ACKNOWLEDGEMENTS

Acknowledgements are due to the editors of the following magazines in which a number of these poems first appeared: *Acumen, Ambit, Chronicles* (USA), *Encounter, The London Magazine, Poetry Review, Shenandoah* (USA), *Spectator, The Times Literary Supplement;* also to Faber & Faber, publishers of *First and Always: Poems for Great Ormond Street Children's Hospital*, in which 'Talking Head' was first published, and to the BBC.

To Martin Reed

Contents

ESCAPOLOGIST

The year was nineteen-thirty,
The place, Eccles.
In the market square, on cobbled stones,
Dark and slimed from recent rain,
Two men had drawn
A few spectators in a ring
Around the space where one
Would now perform.
His skin was pale,
A bluish white, the pallor of boiled cod.
The arms were thin and muscles unheroic.
Those who looked on
Swapped shifty glances,
Wore the same uneasy grin.
An old cloth cap, for pennies, yawned in mud.
The man's assistant manacled his wrists;
Both feet were chained
And he was lowered to the ground
And wrapped from neck to feet
Inside a canvas shroud, then firmly strapped.

The long thin bundle lay
Trussed tight, the head
The only part of him in sight.
And then his struggle to escape began.
Those swivelling eyes were not theatrical;
This thing was real. I read
The language of imprisonment and fear
As that stained, capitate, long parcel
Jerked and bucked and squirmed
In dirt, on obdurate stone.

A few spectators left
And, as they walked away,
The small explosions of their grins,
Becoming laughter, flared, then sputtered out.
And still he wrestled, writhed and fought;
His face contorted, broke beneath the strain:
Those eyes could burst;
Spittle laced the jagged mouth.
This was the face of someone who could die,
A parody of death and birth.

And now, though half a century has passed,
Something of my fear can still defy
Reason and the years,
And I remember how, when he at last
Threw the canvas cloak and chains aside
And sucked in liberal air,
The witnesses did not applaud,
Though some of them threw pennies in the cap,
That few, if any, could afford.

FRYING TONIGHT

Outside, the dark breathes vinegar and salt;
The lemon window seems to salivate,
Draws peckish kids, black moths to candlelight.

Inside you may sit down to eat, or take
Your parcelled supper out into the night.
On each white halo of a china plate

Dismembered golden dactyls form a nest
About the scab of batter which, when split,
Confesses flesh as white as coconut.

Beneath investigation of bright fork
The naked body breaks and separates,
Unfolds its steaming leaves, in smooth soft flakes.

Sleek, plump bottles, bodies almost black
Hold vinegar on all the table tops
Like little holy sisters in white caps.

And on the counter in a gallon can,
Floating blindly in translucent brine,
Small green dirigibles loll still, becalmed.

Those silver vats behind, they all contain
Hot lakes of oil: when fresh peeled chips are drowned
They spit and sizzle like a thousand cats.

In front a patient congregation stands;
These serious communicants who long
To feel warm parcels solid in their hands.

Later, at home, replete, they may spread out
Stained paper cerements, read about old scores,
Dead scandals, weddings, unimportant wars.

BOBBIE

'We used to drink Green Goddesses', she said.
'I don't suppose you even know the name.
At least you've heard of Pimm's. He had a red
MG, my boyfriend did. We'd go to Thame
And stay at Fothergill's pub, the famous one,
Or else nip down to somewhere by the sea
And spend the day just idling in the sun.
And when the long and lovely night began
We'd leave the bar and go outside where we,
And maybe one or two new chums, would dance
There on the esplanade to music from
A gipsy barrel-organ. Such romance
You can't believe, and all along the prom
Coloured lanterns glowed like fairyland.
We'd dance and dance, my dear, and all the time
You'd smell the seaside smell of sea and sand
Behind the lilac, honeysuckle, lime
And *Passing Clouds*, and there, below the sound
Of tango, waltz and foxtrot, you could hear
The hush and sigh of breakers on the strand

And suck and gurgle underneath the pier.
Things were different then, sheer poetry dear;
Such gorgeous lingerie we used to wear.
My boy friends, every one a gentleman;
You'd never hear one raise his voice or swear,
Not like today. Oh, things were different then.
My escort never came without some flowers
And chocolate liqueurs, nice things like that.
They were the days of sunshine and sweet showers,
The dancing days of silver saxophones
And roses.

        Well, thank you for our chat
And for the drinkie too. It's time to go.'
The lipstick marking where her mouth had been
Curved slightly upward at each end although
Her eyes remained unchanged, glass splinters, green,
Like Christmas-cracker jewellery, the gleam
Not quite derisive, watchful, undeceived,
Not asking to be wanted, but believed.

THE PARTY'S OVER
A *Kind of Elegy*

Some years ago – forty or so, I'd guess –
Among the literati of the day
It was fashionable to praise the pure *simplesse*
Of the artist's eye, and you would hear them say
In The Fitzroy or Wheatsheaf, or write in some review,
How the painter or poet with his innocent eye
Perceived a world rinsed by primeval dew,
And marvelled like a child. Maybe. But I
Was never quite convinced although I knew
Of poets, painters and composers who,
Outside the practice of their art, would be
Judged as, if not 'childlike', 'immature'.
One, a poet, died quite recently,
Whose bloodshot vision no one would call 'pure',
And yet he wrote with passion and some wit
And made his own bleak music from despair,
Snarling at life, as if he hated it,
Those obloquies a kind of putrid prayer.
His last appearance, just before he died,
Was at a party given by a friend
Whom he had known for years, and there he tried
To squeeze more from the night than it contained,
Growing more excited with each drink
Frantic for affection and applause.
The less indulgent guests would purse and shrink,
And even his kind host was seen to pause
Before responding to appeals for more
Booze, and love, and flattery.

                    At length
The first departing guests moved to the door;
Soon others followed, sensing that the strength
Which welded this occasion's symmetry
Had suddenly begun to leak away.
'The party's over', someone said; but he,
The ageing poet, was resolved to stay:
'The party isn't over! Mustn't be!'
Indignation and entreaty brimmed his eyes;
His look was like a child's of two or three,
Grey hair and ravaged face, a slipped disguise.
'It isn't over yet!' he cried again.
'Oh yes it is', they said, and made him go
Out into the night of grown-up men
Who laugh, and wave, and slam car-doors and know
The safe road home.
                    Last seen, the poet stood
Blanched and isolated in the chill
Blaze of headlamps, as if carved in wood,
Almost like a winter tree, until
The silver glitter of his piss began,
Rose arching from his centre to descend
On unaffronted hollyhocks and on
A world where all the parties had to end.

THE LARKIN ROOM

A Larkin Room is to be established
at the University Library.

TLS

The walls subfusc with age and nicotine,
Their floral pattern only just
Discernible behind the solid haze;
Two wooden chairs, a table in between,
And in grey air the scent of dust,
As music from a hidden speaker plays.

Bechet, or King Oliver perhaps,
Jazz certainly. The littered books
Are all in English: fiction, mainly light;
Sly female wit and rough stuff from the chaps
Who write of race-courses and crooks;
Nothing even mildly recondite.

Of twentieth century poetry you'll find
Owen, Betjeman, Auden, all
Well-fingered, loved, and, by the narrow bed,
The poems of Thomas Hardy which divined
A wilderness that should appal,
Yet play a marvellous music in the head.

The table holds a saucer-souvenir,
A pair of cycle-clips and sprawl
Of scrawled-on paper, pens, elastic-bands,
And from the ceiling's centre, like a tear,
A single light-bulb hangs; one wall
Displays a photograph of Frinton Sands.

The curtains, faded like a slattern's skirts,
Conspire to keep the daylight out;
They almost meet, not quite, for one is short,
Permits thin gleam of sunlight in to flirt
With dancing dust-motes' prickly rout,
But makes no promises of any sort.

MATCHES

I saw him often, so often that I ceased,
Almost, to notice him. So now I visualize
A photograph or something like a still
From an old movie, shot in black-and-white.
The mood is one of darkness, but not night.
Rain grizzles. It is probably November.
He is standing near the entrance to the Underground
Outside Victoria Station with his tray
Of matches no one buys, though once or twice,
A hurrying traveller drops a coin or two
On to the tray. He wears a burglar's cap
And overcoat discarded by a man
Of greater size. Suspended from his neck
A grimy cardboard sign rests on his chest
That few have stopped to read, and written there,
In faded capitals, is this: KID FRANCIS,
LIGHTWEIGHT CHAMPION OF THE WORLD, NOW BLIND.
The picture does not show the scenes behind
The stony pupils of his eyes, nor can
We know what those clubbed ears may listen to
From peopled darkness in the stadium
Beyond the white-drenched altar of the ring.
Perhaps a kind of mercy operates,
Prevents his seeing what this world is like,
In which a king is brought to beggary,
And almost everyone is blind to him.

ACCESS TO THE CHILDREN

The polar bears are sculpted lumps of snow.
If they feel sympathy it doesn't show.
The monkeys are absorbed in their own business;
Their nimble, unrestrained indecencies
May or may not express contempt for those
Who watch uneasily or move away
With furtive eyes to where the zebras stay
Quite still, great dusty humbugs on four stilts,
No more concerned than that giraffe who tilts
And sways in useless camouflage and shakes
His high disdainful head above the groups
Or pairs, the Sunday fathers and their young,
The sullen sons and daughters, little troops
Of conscripts, heirs to marital mistakes,
Their pouting faces blubbered, rouged and stung
By cold and petulance. Each father's grin
Has frozen to a desperate grimace.
He wonders if he'll be invited in
When they get back to what was once his place,
Deciding to refuse with some excuse
In case he finds that he will have to face
His smug usurper's patronizing gaze.

At last the withered daylight starts to fade
And darkens like a leaf. It's time to go.
The children, sick from sweets and lemonade,
Trail toward the gates to start the slow
Journey to the Underground and home.
Early lamps throw bars of yellow light
Across the path, and spectres of the reek
Of stale captivity steal through the night,
Lingering like smoke in hair and clothes,
And will not disappear next day, or week.

ELAINE'S STORY

This happened when I was eight years old.
I was wearing my silver bracelet
That Grannie gave me for my birthday.
Mummy was not there. I did not know
Where she had gone. It was a dark day
And it smelled of Monday. In the hall
The telephone started to ring. And ring.
Daddy was at home. I don't know why.
He was a policeman then. Not now.
He stays at home and looks after us.
I saw him pick up the telephone.
Yes, he said, Yes. He said it again.
Then he said, I see. I don't think
He could see though. His eyes were like glass
Or more like ice. They began to melt
And I saw his face starting to break.
The pieces did not fall on the floor
But they did not seem to fit together
Like they ought to do. I felt frightened.
His face is better now, looks mended
But not the same. His eyes don't either.
Mummy did not come back home. I kept
Asking where she was but now I've stopped.
I've stopped asking anything. Grannie
Said she is with Jesus and happy.
I pretended that I believed her.

SNOWFALL AT NIGHT

The slow and spectral dance is on:
Seven million tiny veils, each one
Frail as a martyred leaf, begin
Their blind work of hypnosis;
And all is so mysterious,
And most mysterious of all,
The more than silence of the fall.

Now, at the window your warm brow
Is sluiced by coolness of the glass,
And sarabands of flakes endow
The heart and eyes with ease; alas,
An ease that, like the fall, will pass.

So these slow gestures of the snow
Bestow a present from the past,
Enchantment close to innocence
Which, like the whiteness, cannot last.

WATERING THE FLOWERS

Week upon week of heat,
A summer that the young
Are spellbound by and grateful for,
And we, the old,
Remember from a long-ago Arcadia;
No rain for many days:
The garden soil is cindery with the need
For fresh, celestial waters, healing draughts.
And so I come,
Watering-can in hand,
To ease distress of hyacinth,
Peony, heart's-ease, dahlia and rose,
And they lift grateful faces to the spray,
Silvery and cool,
From my beneficent hand.
They think that I am God.
I care for them in their bright parishes;
I send their roots rain.

Later, lapped in lamplight,
Implicated in
A cello's lovely lucubrations
In the key of C,
I think about the flowers,
Their possible theology,
And wonder what satanic image might
Perturb their peace:
A biped, like their God? Like me?
Though one not bringing sustenance
But bending over them
To cloak the sun and cast a gloom
In whose grim shadow gleam
Steel blades to cut their slender throats?

Or could it be
A quadruped that squats and squirts
Envenomed rain and buries bones
In their dark place of genesis?

LACRIMAE RERUM

Whatever is remembered and preserved
In photographic images or words,
In music or those spectral, yet unblurred,
Pictures that may flower inside the head,
However bright, faint shades of loss intrude,
Presences of tears, unshed or shed.

One summer night I walked across the Heath,
Alone and lonely, even then past youth;
The moon gleamed white and curved, a tiger's tooth.
And then, surprising as a starburst, came
Those voices calling to me from the gloom,
Inviting me to step into a dream:

A midnight feast; young men and girls had spread
White linen on the grass, on this displayed
Wine, fruit, various meats and bread.
They were servants from a neighbouring hotel,
Italians, Spaniards, Cypriots, as well
As waitresses from Leeds and Liverpool.

They welcomed me to share their food and wine;
Their friendliness was absolute, it shone
More brightly than the moon's apprentice shine;
We shared, not only nourishment, but bliss,
Yet even in that glade of blessedness
A brackish hint of dawn soon chilled the grass.

Another scene: inside a hotel room;
Jalousies are shut against the sun,
A noon of sensual delights, perfume
And cream of skin, such pungencies!
Gold powder swirls in dusk as voices rise
In contrapuntal music of wild cries.

But, even while love's lexicon
Is rapturously incarnated in
That shadowy room, outside small sounds begin:
Thin whimper of a baby and the sigh
Of rising wind that will, before the day
Is done, bring rain from misanthropic skies.

Now, warm in lamplight on this winter's night
I listen to a Mozart work for flute
And orchestra in D: again I note
How that pure statement just a little aches
With threads of sadness, even in its jokes,
And sigh with pleasure at the noise it makes.

THE BETTER WORD

Bonfire: (orig. bone-fire) a great fire
in which bones were burnt in the open air.
                    Shorter Oxford English Dictionary

Summer's petals shrivel in the cold
And dim atelier of memory;
Their scent is difficult to resurrect.
Sensitive potatoes have grown old;
First sweetness lost, they're stout and coarse, like me;
Their toughened skin is maculate and flecked
With warts and wens. This is a time for fires
In gardens and in grates. Outside, the trees
And shrubs are vague and sorrowful in mist;
Stems of clematis, like tangled wires,
Torment the trellis. Under apple trees
Rotting Bramleys deliquesce when pressed
Beneath my heavy tread. In spite of all
The sodden earth and vaporous air I stack
Branches, twigs, stale news, a magazine,
Some broken toys, aborted poems' stained scrawl,
All things that fire is eager to attack,
Or will be when I splash the paraffin

On wood and paper, add the match's flare,
Like so... Soon leaves of flame fandango, flaunt
And wrangle in the smoke; an ancient scent,
Both sweet and acrid, spices swirling air;
Faint images and far-off speakings haunt
The weather in the skull, all redolent
Of unspecific loss; but then, as plain
As if the child were by my side, I hear
The voice from almost thirty years ago
Of my son, Toby, calling me again
To make a 'grandfire', and the word is clear:
Let's make a grandfire dad! And still I know
As I knew then, that through mishearing or
The infant tongue's recalcitrance he'd found
A better word than 'bonfire' for this blaze
Whose flames are now gone widdershin and roar
And crackle, spitting pips of sparks around,
In truly grand and not ossiverous ways.

LOVE WORD

Taught from his earliest days to be discreet
And lower eyes before this naked word
       He later found
That only in the fumes and huffing heat
Of sexual catch-as-can when vision blurred
    And logic and decorum drowned
    In tidal waves, could he be heard
    To utter that brief liquid sound,
A senseless and involuntary bleat.

Mendacious too, as he will now admit,
Since advent of his children has made clear
       The word's sweet sum,
Yet still he finds he cannot utter it,
Though on two shy occasions in each year,
    While he remains completely dumb,
    He writes on cards and hopes they'll hear
    The single syllable become
Alive for his, not their, dear benefit.

ON THE CHEVIN

November and the rowan berries burn
In brilliant clusters in their dark green caves.
Disgruntled clouds sag low with unshed rain.
The path that runs through now dishevelled woods
Of oak and birch and conifer is mulched
With decadence of fallen leaves on moss
As soft as felt beneath the feet. No dogs
And tumbling summer children to be seen.

A man and woman walk, their pace so slow
It seems to tease the notion of arrival.
The colour of their clothes rhymes with the weather.
This couple is quite unremarkable,
Unless joined hands could waken interest.
Her head tilts slightly to her right and rests
An inch beneath his shoulder, his inclines
Towards her own. They do not seem to speak.

At last the footpath's terminal is reached,
An area where patient cars are parked,
And here they disengage their hands and pause,
Face to face, quite close, though silent still.
The long embrace and kiss don't quite occur.
They turn away to different cars. Doors slam.
Both engines snarl. His car moves off, then hers,
In opposite directions, gathering speed.

THE SPELL

She will not come.
He works with brush and mop and pail, and sees
Suds glitter, deliquescent diamonds, where
The citrous fragrances ascend to please
Grateful nostrils of the morning air;
And yet he says: *She will not come.*

She will not come.
He places flowers in vases to dispose
About the house to sweeten space and light –
Lily, jasmine, emblematic rose –
He trims the lamps in readiness for night,
Yet still he says: *She will not come.*

She will not come
But he puts on his coat, goes out to buy
Honey and brown eggs and wine and bread,
Apples, grapes and cheese and medley pie,
Returns to spread fresh linen on the bed,
But says again: *She will not come.*

She will not come
Collusive twilight veils the brooding skies;
A chill breeze whispers like a distant sea;
He waits in deepening darkness with closed eyes.
As spell against its own fulfilment he
Repeats the words: *She will not come.*

SHE SPEAKS THE WORDS

At last she speaks the words he longed to hear:
Lying in his grateful arms she sighs,
'I love you,' and he looks into her eyes
And sees, in each, the glitter of a tear;
And, when again she breathes the words, he feels
In his euphoria a glint of fear.
The music of her voice is sad, reveals
No trace or echo of his own elation,
And underneath the melancholy steals
A contrapuntal note of accusation.

ANNIVERSARY INTERVIEW

Since you've been partners for so long may I
Face you with a question that you might
Find very difficult indeed to answer.
Are you happily in love with her?
Well, I don't know; the question's made of words.
What happens if I shuffle them like cards?
They turn up meaning something more or less
Significant, though still ambiguous.
In love with her, and *happily*, you said.
That *in* has always seemed a little odd –
In debt, in jail, in terror, in despair –
The preposition seems to chime far more
Matily with bleaker nouns than that
Liquid syllable you'd never shout.
Try *with her happily in love*. It makes
A certain sense, except that *in* still irks;
Or *happily with her in love*. This could
Mean happy me because she loves. I'll spread
The words out one more time and that's the last.
Oh yes, the sequence now makes sense; the best,
The only honest, statement I can make
After all these years; it may sound weak,
But here's the answer your five words now give –
Rip up semantics, syntax and such stuff,
For I am in her, happily, with love.

STUNT DIVER

A jangle of coloured lights, though darkness hissed
Beneath those motionless or spinning glitterings,
The fairground called to us with pounding blare
Of noise and we ran eagerly towards it,
Children of a dying day, our fists
Bunched tight about the pennies we would lose.
1936, the year, though we
Knew nothing of Cordoba, Saragossa
Or Berlin. The fairground was our El Dorado
And there, among the whirling brilliancies,
We saw the tower of scaffolding
With the little platform on the top
Just visible against the glowing sky.
And at the foot a water-tank was set,
Cubiform, not more than twelve feet square,
And, propped against this vat, a blackboard leaned
On which the words were chalked: *'Tonight at 9
Stan Linbergh England's greatest diving ace
Performs his death-defying dive through flames.'*

By nine o'clock a crowd had gathered round
And we had waited patiently to keep
As close as was permitted to the tank.
A small man in a tilted opera hat
Striped with the colours of the Union Jack
Shouted through his conic megaphone,
Exhorting everyone to keep well back
Because the water in the tank would blaze
With dangerous flames when Captain Linbergh dived.
More waiting: then at last the hero came.
'Make way!' the patriot shouted and the crowd
Heaved and rustled as a path was made
For Linbergh to walk through. His head was bowed;

He wore a greatcoat with the collar pulled
About his ears. He looked like one condemned.
He reached the tower, removed his overcoat
And briefly shuddered. We could see the flesh
Of arms and shoulders, legs; and we were shocked
To see how soft and white they looked, not carved
From dark, heroic metal or tough teak
But hurtable, almost a girls' pale limbs.
Then he began to climb.
                          We watched his slow
Insectile progress up the trembling tower
And saw, as he drew closer to the small
Platform at the top, his movements seem
To grow more tentative and slow. But he
At last stood there, transformed by distance to
A manikin, Tom Thumb, a something more
Or less than ordinary man. The crowd
Now held its breath as if it stood up there
And was about to dive, while, on the ground,
His partner swung an arm and shouted out,
'Now keep right back!' and in a second flames
Leapt, blazing from the water in the tank,
And Linbergh dived.

It was no Tarzan dive,
Slow-motion, breasting air with swallow grace
And swooping downwards like a feathered dart;
No: Linbergh dropped, a heavy stone, so fast
We still stared upwards after he had plunged
Through fire into the tank and dowsed the flames
With that explosive crunch. And then he rose
Shaking water-shrapnel from his head,
And heaved his glistening body from the tank
And climbed down to safe earth. He raised one hand
Acknowledging the patter of applause,
And then put on his coat. His partner moved
Among the crowd, his upturned hat become
A begging-bowl.
　　　　　We did not move away,
Held there by an unreasonable sense
Of being cheated: there must be more to come.
Stan Linbergh and his partner had both gone;
The dark mass of the crowd began to break
And crumble, trickling off towards the lights
And noises of the roundabouts and stalls.
At last we, too, turned slowly from that place
And with a single backward glance we left,
Not speaking, sulky with the sense of loss,
Robbed of something none of us dared name.

AFTERNOON MEN

'... drunkards, afternoon-men, and such as
more than ordinarily delight in drink ...'
          [Burton. The Anatomy of Melancholy]

What has happened to the afternoon-men
Now that the afternoon clubs have closed?
They shawled themselves in twilight when
The sun was bright and the old folk dozed
On benches in the public park;
Each sought his own dim, pungent den
And drank in that expensive dark.

While serious people worked away
In office, factory, shop or field,
The afternoon-men went in to play;
They slouched or shuffled, lurched or reeled
Through doors that knew their shadows well –
The *Mandrake, Caves, ML* – to stay
And drink till they, or darkness, fell.

The *Marie Lloyd*, known as plain *ML*
By the afternoon-men, was a paradigm
Of all such clubs: pervasive smell
Of stale tobacco, patina of grime
On the walls and floor; and, on the bar,
Filled ashtrays and fake asphodel:
A babble of noise like a small bazaar.

Failed scholars, ponces, purblind seers;
Poets, sepia with nicotine:
Rayner, Ruthven and their peers,
Louis and Terence, would all convene
Daily with their thespian mates,
Felix and Pat, whose furtive fears
Would soon be realized in their separate fates.

They have all gone into the world of dark,
The wise, the witty, the dumb and the trite;
Charon has welcomed them on to his barque –
It was all a rehearsal for the last night.
The doors of the Clubs are locked and the rust
Forms in the wards and the message is stark:
The afternoon-men have been joined with the dust.

WATCHING THE CRICKET

Sun simmers in a gentian sky,
White blossoms of small clouds hang still
Above the elms, in whose spread stain
       Of shadow go
Plump and strutting pigeons. High
Above the trees two skylarks spill
Their sparkling note like silver grain
       On us below.

White flash and smack of ball on bat;
A shout, and like a frightened thing,
Scurrying on hidden paws
       Across the green,
The ball is chased; a soft white hat
Spins down, a dove with broken wing;
We hear small flutter of applause:
       You have the scene.

Now note that bench where three old men
Sit and watch and rarely say
More than a muttered word except
       To show dismay
And some contempt, recalling when
They were young enough to play,
How keen they'd been and more adept
       In every way.

Then, after tea, as shadows grow
Longer on the grass, the old
Men speak even less and their
      Eyes half close;
How much they see is hard to know,
Or if the little hint of cold,
Glinting in the evening air,
      Disturbs their doze.

It's almost close of play, and they
Surely hear the umpire cry
The final 'Over!' If they do
      They only yawn
And stretch and, when they turn away,
Seem not to see, as day must die,
Their separate nights are beckoning too,
      As stumps are drawn.

SECOND SIGHT

Poor eyesight has its compensations,
allows access to a world whose furniture
surprises. I remove my glasses
as I walk with my whippet
in the summer park and, instantly, she melts
into the green earth and disappears.
Irked by her continued absence I begin
to whistle and to call her by name,
and I am again startled
at her small yelp as I stumble over her.

I am gulled by the scattered white stones
which suddenly ascend and punish the air
with slapping wings. The beautiful girl,
as in Greek myth, is changed
by my proximity into a laurel.
A fallen paper bag starts to bark.
In the distance I see trees as men talking.
I resume my spectacles,
expecting the commonplace.
It is revealed, rinsed with recent theurgy.

SHADOW ON THE SNOW

The old man wore a gown of morning light.
Through silvery translucence and against
Smooth ermine hiding wintry grass from sight
He felt his scarecrow body, gaunt and flensed.

He looked up at the sky, as cleansed and blue
As on the morning of its making; no
Smudge of cloud or wink of wing; a new
World fashioned by the legerdemain of snow.

But he was old; the same warped gallows frame;
Yet, on the white before him, strode the tall
Figure, soldierly, erect, not lame,
Impervious to pain, not aged at all.

GROWING OLD

The sheer incredibility thumps hard
        And sharp; he's stunned,
      And then, instinctively, he reaches
For pockets, digging deep to find his fund
      Of verbal amulets that guard
Against the cruel lessons that time teaches.

He says he feels no older than he did
        At twenty-one:
      It's almost true, at times completely;
And while the magistrate could be his son –
      Though that he should be, God forbid! –
His crimes are juvenile and sing as sweetly.

Of course he must admit he's short of wind.
        From time to time
      Images in unexpected
Mirrors in the bar or shop will mime
      And mock his looks when double-chinned
Gross parodies are cruelly reflected.

The mechanism in the skull is not
        In-perfect nick.
      And there are times when it remembers
Events that did not happen, yet will stick
      At some impenetrable spot
As dark as a revolver's empty chambers.

The innocence of children makes him cry,
Their faces, eyes,
The way they smile, that trust and candour.
Time and the world prepare their bleak surprise,
The knowledge that we all must die
In disappointment, pain or feeble anger.

And strangely, he is also touched to see
The very old,
The way they fumble in worn purses,
And how their gnarled and brittle fingers hold
The quarter-pound of cheapest tea
With all the care of dedicated nurses.

His dog, he thinks, will probably survive
His own farewell:
If so his soul will briefly linger,
Faint echo of his voice, a fading smell,
In ears and muzzle, just alive
Until displaced by neutralizing hunger.

And yet today, an ordinary day,
Though he walks slow
That gait conceals a lively dancer,
For he is happier now than years ago
When, melancholy's frequent prey,
He dredged each long night's dark, and found no answer.

ADVENT

From the back doorstep, seen through steam
Of mist powdered with faint fall
Of drifting rain,
Square lozenges of yellow gleam
Against the blackened schoolhouse wall.
Though it is morning, lamplight floods each pane.

Beyond the windows children sit
At little desks. I hear and see
And even smell
The scene as I imagine it,
Or conjure it from memory,
Self-enthralled by this deliberate spell.

It is the last month of the year
Bedecked in coloured paper-chains
With tinselled hair,
Dispensing artificial snow. I hear,
Or almost hear, the treble strains
Of carols sweetening the studious air.

I see the faces, which are one,
Girl or boy, multiplied:
Each wears the same
Rapt smile and gleaming hair, fine-spun
And weightless cap of gold; the wide
And wondering gaze in light of candle flame.

I turn away, go back inside
To kitchen warmth and shut the door:
An old man's room,
Populous with shades; a hide
For revenants whose nightly spoor
Trail slender silver ribbons through the gloom.

The children's eyes and voices press
Inside the borders of recall
Insisting on
An innocence, no more or less
Authentic than my ghosts' thin scrawl
Whose meaning I decline to brood upon.

FADING AWAY

As frail as wedding veils lace curtains float
Inside the bedroom window, swirl and swell
Bellying, exhale and then retreat,
Pause tremulous above the ledge until
Another boastful flourish is impelled
By floral breath of summer, cool and sweet.

This girlish dancing of the curtains mocks
The masculinity which governs here:
The polished shoes and boots arranged on racks,
The monkish dressing-gown hung on the door,
Framed photograph of his old brigadier,
Piled copies of the *Tatler* in neat stacks.

The Colonel's daughter, Joan, and Mrs Beese,
Take turns to sit with him. For them these days
Are long but not, Joan thinks, for him who lies
In drugged and sunless limbo – yet who knows
What images might terrify or tease
Behind the sculpted lids of those closed eyes?

That night, her daily tour of duty done,
Joan lies between stiff sheets and cannot sleep:
The little bedside lamp that she keeps on
Paints figures on the walls; there's no escape
From what awaits to sidle close then leap
With cudgel, blade, or blunt and loaded gun.

She is afraid. Her bedroom is not safe:
It's strange, those childish pictures on the wall,
Books and trinkets from another life;
She's often heard it said that people feel
The same at forty as they did when small.
Not her. The future's glinting like a knife.

She switches off the bedside light and hears
Dark silence seeping through from father's room,
Exhausted ocean that no longer roars;
She longs to drown in that warm flood and dream
Reversals of the images of doom
And carnage from his lost, unholy wars.

And sleep, at last, she does till morning calls
With avian scratchings on the window pane;
She stirs and wakes, and instantly she feels
Convinced that he has gone. She is alone
And will, her mirror tells her, so remain,
Attentive to the crunch of carriage wheels.

ON THE MELTON MOWBRAY TRAIN

His book is open; he seems to read
But his deceitful eyes are in fact
Fixed on the grey woman opposite.
He watches her with a kind of greed,
Not for what she is now in the act
Of denuding – a banana – but
Something less innocent. She wears steel-
rimmed spectacles; behind the lenses
Her eyes almost squint as she inclines
Her head towards her tall, pallid meal.
His own lips open as it enters
Her mouth. He lowers his eyes, resigns
Himself to the calmer diversion
Of literature and, as he does so,
He reflects, with only mild surprise,
That, in senescence's bleak season,
He appears, if anything, to grow
More prone to impure thoughts, not wiser
But nastier.
         His destination
Reached, he leaves the train, sets out to go
Into the town, pleased with his disguise,
Bufferish, genteel, and all it hides,
Where they breed horses and make pork pies.

OLD SHAVER

I am surprised by how young I look
In the mirror, now it is misted by steam.
It is true I have removed my spectacles
And the mirror is of such circumference
That my defoliated skull is not revealed.
This simulacrum of youth does not greatly perturb;
Its mild mockery is not malicious.
The unambiguous script of wrinkles, and the furrows
Carved deep, like cicatrix, are smoothed away;
Even the whites of the eyes have lost
Their rubineous glaze.
                I do not stay
And stare for long, but address myself
To what I am here to do. I beard my jowls
With snowy foam, then coax, with keen steel,
Protestant bristles from my jaws and chin.
This operation done I rinse and dry,
Replace my spectacles to face the day,
And what is there, and always had to be.

THE OTHER WORD

Confluence of contradictions are contained
In the weft of the word: soft scrolls of mist,
Infusion of swan's feathers, white hush
Hovering over unfathomable dusk,
Slow griefs of watchers gowned in wax,
The sleeping head sunk in snow,
Filled by the pillow; the hidden hand
Swinging the bell to bring the children in;
Light drained from the looking-glass;
Silence when all breathings cease;
Padlocked iron gates, the green pagodas
Unstirred by erotetic breeze, by breath,
That single and defiant rhyme;
Here is something to be knelt before,
Acknowledged tutelage of love,
Sable regency and, over all,
That mercy, inexorable and pure.

AIDE-MÉMOIRE

Must not forget: write to Martha Frame.
But no. I'll telephone. It costs about the same.

Write that review for the TLS.
I've read most of the book – well, more or less.

Prepare my lecture for the 23rd.
Rough notes will do. They won't listen to a word.

And write, I really must, to Terence Snow.
Oh Jesus Christ, I can't! He died four months ago!

It's terrible how quickly we forget,
How cruelly ephemeral the pain and the regret.

Last week I thought of Iris, quite by accident –
The name on a seed-packet – and I recalled her scent

And the way she smiled as she peeped through her hair,
As if from behind a curtain, both shy and debonair.

And only last night I thought of Ivan and Fred,
Shot down over Hamburg. For five decades they've been dead,

But I hadn't thought of either for many years,
And, when at last I did, it was with more fear than tears.

Some faces and names are forgotten, I must confess,
All sucked away into that black hole of nothingness

Where all must go, including me, I'm afraid,
To linger briefly in a living mind or two, then fade.

So now I think of those words from a poem still dear to me:
'Memory fades, must the remembered perishing be?'.

TELEGRAM

Logic, grammar, each grey vocable
Broke into pieces when the telegram
Fell from her faint fingers, dainty bomb
Exploding on the carpet like a bubble.

No punctuation, though beyond the glass
Of veiled french-windows could be seen a few
Dark circumflexes printed on the sky
And yellow commas scattered on the grass.

Mummy was distraught and Daddy proud,
Each isolated in parentheses.
Silent exclamations marked her cheeks,
But he stood staring at a distant cloud,

Private, pleasurable to contemplate.
He almost smiled. Never had she felt
Such hatred for the man, or so much guilt
Remembering her son and her delight

And pride reflecting his exuberant joy
In those twin asterisks that gleamed upon
Each epaulette: her own sweet subaltern,
Unchangeably her gentle, aureate boy.

At least she cannot see him now he lies,
A black full-stop punched neat between white eyes.

OWL FACES

An early autumn night; the leaves are still;
No whispered bedtime legends to be told;
In huddled clusters apples gleam, pale gold;
The moon-washed air is motionless until,
As if the moon itself must now confess
A sadness it has struggled to withold,
It publishes aloud its loneliness.

As that cool ululation soars and dives,
Small sonic meteor, across the skies,
The echo lingers and, before it dies,
A yet more plaintive twin of it contrives
To follow down the track the first has scored:
Its plangency and echo emphasise
How almost perfect silence is restored.

And in the darkness underneath the trees
Recent windfalls nestle in the grass;
The skin of each is smooth and cold as glass;
And you may lift up any one of these
And carry it indoors and take a bright
Knife and halve, then quarter it, to face
Four faces staring from their unlocked night.

NIGHT OUT

...And when Night
Darkens the Streets, then wander forth the Sons
Of Belial, flown with insolence and wine.
                    Paradise Lost, Book One

Saturday and early evening;
In little houses, where savoury phantoms
Lurk on the stairs, the lads are busy
At kitchen sink or bathroom basin;
They scrape and rinse and titivate, annoint
Their skins with famous unguents and choose
Carefully the clobber for the coming night.

Obedient muscles swell, blue serpents writhe.
They decorate their limbs with bracelets and frail
                                        chains.
Mums are kissed or carelessly *tarrahed*;
Then out to where the town lies welcoming,
Perhaps a little scared but open wide,
They wander forth, rehearse their shouts.
The bars wear necklaces of lights, like girls.

Blue scarves of smoke unfurl and swirl;
The juke-box thrashes silence till it howls;
Torn mouths shout mad hosannas. Soon
The lights will die. Last Orders has been called.
The doors are open and the pavement feels
The crack and splash of noisy yellow streak
Across its dark and sweating face of stone.

Back to the streets: glass trembles to be smashed.
Buttocks, white as Wensleydale, are bared
To mock the moon; moonstruck they roar
And swill from can and slurp from polystyrene,
Swallowing their venomous viatica.
Blue flashes whirl their whining whips
And compound fractures whimper in the dirt.

Sunday, and a grey, exhausted quiet
Lies on the morning streets; the asphalt
Advertises jaundiced asterisks of puke
And crumpled cans and jagged bottle shards.
Church-bells begin to toll, lugubrious,
And those few worshippers who venture out
Move on slow, mournful feet, as to a funeral.

BUSH VET

That's what they call me. Know what it means?
A veteran of Nam, that's vee-et-nam,
You might have heard of it. It's history now.
The bush, that's where I live,
Up there. You see the trees against the sky,
The forest on the hillside like a pelt?
That's home for me,
Miles away from any living soul.
I come down here
Maybe once a month, or less than that,
To get supplies, oil for the lamp,
Coffee, cans of beans and stuff,
Whisky and tobacco, chiefly them.
A couple, maybe three times, in a year
I get to come in here and hang one on,
Not for company you understand.
I don't get lonely in the bush.
It's other folk, like those guys over there,
That make you feel the loneliness come down.
No sir, I got no need of company,
I like it fine up there.
When I first picked the place
So long ago,
I can't recall exactly when,
I fixed a kind of bivouac.
I slept in that while building me a shack.
It took a while but I'd got time enough.
It don't look great, but keeps the weather out,
And other things. There's memories of Nam
I just can't talk about. Bad things.

I think a lot and sometimes I read books,
That's when I'm feeling tidy in my head,
When I can concentrate. Mostly though
I dream about what was and might have been.
But here's a crazy thing I'll tell you now:
After I got back from Nam
And got my discharge, tried to settle down,
I couldn't make it. Mostly couldn't sleep
And if I did, oh man, the dreams I had.
But here's the crazy part. I missed it all.
I wanted to get back – well, part of me –
I dreamed about the palm groves and the paddies,
The water buffalo, the bamboo hills,
The wooden ploughs the oxen used to pull,
The peasants working in the fields,
The elephant grass that sliced you like a knife,
The leeches, mud and shit, the fear.
Even that.
I got depressed, got mad. I couldn't help it.
Couple a drinks and I could kill,
Kill anyone you understand.
I had to get away.
I'm safe up there.
There's water near my shack, a stream.
I don't need halizone for that.
Truth is I'm just not fit for anything,
I mean for living in a city,
Or anywhere with ordinary folk.
I seen too many killed, too many kids
And women, little children, cooked alive.

I seen too much. I need to clean my eyes,
My hands as well. I never will.
In the bush up there I'm safe, I'm tame.
If any human being does get shot
That person will be me. By friendly fire.
That's what they called it when a guy
Got wasted by a buddy's careless stray.
They called it friendly fire.
It happened all the time. And what the hell
Difference does it make, a VC slug
Or M14, you end up dead the same.
I sometimes wish I had.
There's some things I don't want to ask myself,
And yet the questions sneak up in the night
And grab you by the throat. Or should I say
The question there's no hiding from.
What was it for?
The killing and the fear, the suffering, the shit?
What was it for? And if the question's bad
The answer's worse. Nothing. That's the word.
You know what nothing is?
Nothing is a hole with nothing in it,
A round black emptiness with nothing round it,
A hole punched in a human skull,
When all the flesh has rotted, gone.
Nothing is the muzzle of a gun,
Dark centre of a whirlpool made of steel,
The dark beyond the dark.
Emptiness beyond all emptiness,
Silence under silence,
Nothing is the answer to it all.

IN MEMORIAM C.M.H.

There are many days when I never think about him.
I do not apologize, nor would he wish me to,
And I write this to gratify a quite selfish whim:
Having no picture of him I shall have to make do
With this rough sketch when his memory grows dim:
One of a dying species from the human zoo.

He was lean and fierce and could stun you with a surprise
Weapon of geniality. His rages would make
Walls tremble like virgins; tusks menaced, and from his eyes
Flashed sizzling tracers, but after each violent quake
The peace it left was like the calm when a great storm dies
And his smile came sweet and white as a wedding-cake.

He believed in capital punishment, but not in God.
He loved his wife, gave her expensive presents and hell.
Each evening at exactly half-past-six he would plod
Upstairs to take his bath. At seven a tactful smell
Of soap ushered him into his study where he stood
Sinking a double whisky before the dinner knell.

I use 'knell' not merely for the rhyme. He made each meal
A grave occasion and like a mad pathologist
He dissected his food, probing with mistrustful zeal
For evidence of crime. Gloom and silence like a mist
Shrouded the feast. Then he swallowed his ritual pill
And belched, swore and muttered like a drunk ventriloquist.

Each morning he rose at precisely seven o'clock
To perform calisthenics for which he was too old.
His bones were like dead branches over which a loose smock
Of dried flesh was hung. Not for decades had muscles rolled
Under that wizened skin. Yet we felt no wish to mock
His strenuous folly, nor dared we attempt to scold.

He had fought at Mons and Wipers. In seventy-four,
One evening of reminiscing, his musings strayed
Back to his army days; then he asked about my war,
Had I enjoyed it? I said I would sooner have stayed
At home. Those times, for me, were frightening or a bore.
He said, 'I don't know what it feels like to be afraid.'

And I believed him. He was vain, bigoted and brave,
Tyrannical, a great snob. He often made me wild.
I should have hated him, but I did not. He gave
Prodigally of love, hate and cash. Often reviled
He stood firm by his views. And now he is in the grave
Grief multiplies for one, part father and friend, part child.

FOUR ROYS

It is a curious, if fairly obvious, fact
That people, celebrated or quite unknown,
Seem to grow into their christian names, expand or contract
According to whether they should be seven or seventeen stone.
But it's not as simple as that. A christian name
Generally regarded as dull, or even absurd,
May be alchemized by a great possessor's fame
Into something noble and ennobling; this has occurred
For instance with Poets Laureate – though by no means all –
With Alfred (Tennyson, not Austin) a name
Was rescued from the dandruffy drab and became,
Briefly, royal again. William, a name that few would call
Especially resonant before its conjunction with Wordsworth
                                        (not Whitehead)
Grew soberly strong; those like Naham, Cecil, and Colley
Are condemned. like their owners, to the ranks of the benighted
Or recalled, if at all, as embodiments of vanity and folly.
God alone knows what posterity will make of Ted.

Now, all of these generalizations about Christian names
Are a windy prelude to a fragmentary recollection
Of four acquaintances, two of them now dead,
All of them bearing the first name of Roy,
Three of them practitioners of the art of versification
And one I have not seen since I was a boy
And will not see again who, if he felt the temptation
To make poems, resisted it. What he *did* make
Was model aeroplanes. I envied him this skill.
His ambition, which neither mockery nor mother could shake,
Was to be a bomber pilot. He would never fulfil
His other longing – to be one of Greyfriars' Famous Five,
Preferably Harry Wharton, though I think he would have settled
Even for Billy Bunter – which could never come alive,
Except in imagination, of course. though once, when nettled
He actually shouted. 'I say, you beastly cad!' and this
Was in the playground of Queen's Park Council School
Where everyone was too astonished to take the piss.

Most of us regarded him as a kind of holy fool.
His other dream, though, was briefly fleshed. He died in flames
In flak-ripped skies over Berlin. The other dead one
Was killed in 1957 in a car-crash in Spain.
He and I were not close friends, each fed on
Quite different ideological and literary grub
Though we did share one experience: together we were thrown
Out of the Windsor Castle, not the royal seat but a pub
In Notting Hill Gate. He had a reputation
For being a fighting man based chiefly, it seemed to me,
On reports of a small altercation
He had with a fellow poet not known for his ferocity.
I found him soft and mild though of substantial size.
He wrote some blustering satire and sweet lyrics but translation
Was his true strength: he made fine versions of one of God's great spies,
St John of the Cross, of Lorca and of Baudelaire.

About the two living Roys I have little to say,
Knowing neither very well. Enough that they both care
Seriously for their craft and each in his own way
Has written poems that delight and go on delighting.
The prospect of sharing a compartment with either or both
On a long railway journey would be distinctly inviting.
Well – where was I? – oh yes, names. To tell the truth
I'd forgotten what I was supposed to be on about –
Christian names: four men, three poets and one not,
All named Roy. Not a strong name. It is without
Power, despite its echo of 'King'. It would suit a swot,
Someone neat and correct, or a senior boy-scout.

It is not, as the young might say, much of a turn-on,
Though, come to think of it, I can't imagine what,
They would have to say about the christian name Vernon –
Who could wear comfortably such a name? What kind of man?
I can't think what they'd say. Or perhaps I can.

DYLAN THOMAS COUNTRY

A bowl of seasons at the hills' feet,
    A helmet of weathers;
At night the white owl, fat and shining,
Blinks among scattered crumbs and trinkets
    And the sleepless sea
Over and over sighs and surrenders.

This day decides on rising to sport summer;
    It comes out dancing;
The green dress shimmers with relucent beads;
Little houses and enormous horses
    Whinny their waking;
Trout practise their scales in the waterfall pool.

In this country, and in all but one season,
    A plump boy
With apple cheeks where no worm burrows
Whistles and wonders with blue amazement
    At the mystery and joy,
The promise of this day and all its fellows.

And should the next day wake up as winter
    Its snow will be sweet
On the tongue, friendly to toes and fingers,
Chilblains glow only in the evening sky,
    Complected with darkness
To parcel the mistletoe, the evergreen and manger.

The circus of Spring then dazzles the hamlet
    With trumpets and flags;
The laughter of daffodils waves to the master,
A chorus of crocuses seasons the singing,
    The big cats roar
But will never molest the boy of Easter.

The fall does not happen at all in this country
    Where uncles are huge
And tremendously gentle and aunts are funny;
No insults, no harpies or hangovers rage,
    No gaol here or factory,
No college of pain, gigantic infirmary.

This country welcomes the rarely enchanted,
    The meagre and sour;
Here they rip off their collars of caution,
Ethical serge, their boots and galoshes,
    They dance and munch flowers
Though the worm eats the face of the boy of Autumn.

FLYING BLIND

Soft, blundering fog has neutralized
The morning sky, and from that foul
And padded air is recognized
The aircraft's stretched catarrhal growl.

A plane about to land, we hope
In safety though, on looking through
Imagination's telescope,
We see that they are hoping too.

And some within that metal case
Dictate a message straight to God;
They stare through glass but only face
The day's enormous smothering wad.

It bandages the windows tight
However much they crane and peer;
Their voices flutter on a bright
Chilly thread of perfect fear.

Everyone becomes a blind
Longing for the feel of earth
Beneath his feet, amazed to find
How much one stepping-stone is worth.

And they are right to be afraid,
Though wrong about the aircraft's fate,
For they should fear the ambuscade
Crouching there beyond the gate.

POETRY NOW

How is it done?
Shift your glass into your left hand;
Drink southpaw for a while;
Lead with the right,
Jab and jab, persistent;
With luck you'll see
The trickle soon become a flow.

Don't get excited and impatient now.
Be resolute
But wary, cool,
And don't be tempted to show off.
Erato is in your corner
Who never tells you why you do it,
But sometimes tells you how.

ENGLISH SUMMER

It's August in England and time for vacation;
A full hour of sunshine would cause a sensation.
The weather's called 'fine' if the rain isn't falling
And few of us curse at the wind's catawauling.
It's usual in Blackpool or Morecambe or Brighton
To crouch in a shelter and watch gulls alight on
The crests of the curling and shit-bearing breakers,
Or bleakly stare out over grey salty acres;
And later, at nightfall, more *forte* than *piano*,
Hear choirs of brass monkeys all singing soprano.

GETTING OVER IT

They said, 'Don't worry: you'll get over it.'
And they were always right; you always did.
The wounds healed up and didn't hurt a bit.

After a time of course. Meanwhile you hid
The fact that you were hurting, or you tried;
Not always easy for a pampered kid:

Disappointments over which you cried –
The model aeroplane that wouldn't fly,
The whispered promises that always lied,

Then stumbling into love, the biggest lie
As things turned out; you thought your heart would break,
But you recovered from it by and by.

And so it rolled – betrayal, belly-ache,
Rejection, blows, a dozen kinds of shit:
There wasn't any kind you didn't take.

When flesh and eyes were sore with dust and grit
You seemed a static target none could miss,
They said, again, that you'd get over it.

And they were right. Though no one told you this –
That on the other side lay the abyss.

TALKING HEAD

Take the unfleshed head, the strict skull;
Hold it in the palm of your left hand
While, with pincers of right forefinger and thumb,
You carefully select a plump, green grape.
Delicately place the grape in the socket
To the left of where the nose once jutted.
If it does not fit perfectly discard it.
Choose another, and another, until you find
One that plugs in snug. Over the twin cavity
Place a black, piratical eye-patch,
Secured by a wide elastic band.
The choice of hat is yours, a beret perhaps,
A tricorne, sou'wester or a large tea-cosy;
Something sporty like a cricket cap or boater;
Nothing, I suggest, explicitly sacerdotal.
Next, into that empty smile, or snarl,
Insert a partly smoked cheroot or half corona.
Then decide on a topic of conversation,
Not too contentious but not tedious either.
Avoid mentioning rivers, bells, masonry and flowers.
Listen carefully and you may be instructed
Though not, I fear, amused or comforted.

HOME MOVIES

We, the guests, sit in pink twilight.
The cosy box we occupy
Is pretty and warm;
We might be dolls,
But we are men and women,
Have eaten well,
Dressed in appropriate uniform.

Flavours, savoury and sweet, still linger
Pleasantly, but what we ate
Is not quite free;
Now is the time
When payment is exacted,
Not cash of course,
But another quite painful fee.

'Painful', perhaps, is over strident
To designate that grey malaise,
Boredom's sick
And stifling ache;
Our ordeal is beginning:
On the screen
The pictures flicker, blur, then click

Sharply into focus, recognized
With gleeful cries: '*Oh look! There's Paul,*
A Proper Mister
Universe!
And that one on the donkey's
Peter's friend
Who fancied George's younger sister.

Wait for this though! This will slay you!
Judy's fancy swallow-dive!
She swallowed half
The swimming-pool!
That's the place we stayed at –
Rather pricey.
Now this will really make you laugh!'

It did. The laughter sounded rather
Less than joyful, but it came,
Enough for Paul,
Our kindly host.
One cure alone for us though:
To see our own
Dear lineaments dancing on that wall.

INTERVIEW WITH THE AUTHOR

'Your oeuvre is not complete. May I suppose
You have a clear conception of its close?'

'I can't foresee the end, and if I knew
I think I'd hide the dénouement from you.'

'Well, what about the origins? How long
Did you reflect, make notes, upon the throng
Of characters and scenes before the act
Itself of starting on the artefact?'

'Longer than you or anyone will know.'

'What you have so far published seems to show
A passion for crude violence and lust
That could be called obsessive. Now, I trust
You will not think me puritanical
In finding much of this mechanical,
And scarcely edifying. Why do you
Make humans beasts or engines, as you do?'

'You are mistaken there. I have no skill
In metamorphosis. My creatures will
Their own behaviour, shape identities.
I made them, yet the paradox is this:
I cannot change their world from what it is.'

'I see. Your characters assume their own
And independent natures. They alone
Determine what events will come to pass?'

'Well, yes. But only certain ones, alas,
Attain autonomy and power, and they –
The wicked – rule and have the final say.'

APOSTATE

He climbs the steps that look like slabs of cheese,
And when the glass doors glide apart he feels
No surprise at all. He enters, sees
How like a statesman's coffin the long desk gleams
And how, behind it, the woman shines and smiles
With eyes and teeth as bright and cold as nails.
The scratched air bleeds an odour, sour and sharp,
The scent of staples; then the drumbeats start
And, with the drumming, a thin high whining noise.
He knows that he was wrong to come. The caves
Were better far than this.
                              The sliding doors
Are now shut fast and, when he turns, he sees
Reflected in the sheet of glass his face
Fragmented by panic and despair.
The woman's smile has gone and left no scar.
The hungry cold outside is sweet as choice.

Erotetic - interrogatory.

Theurgy n. magic by the agency of
good spirits. - miraculous
divine action.